Harbin Ice and Snow Festival

by Grace Hansen

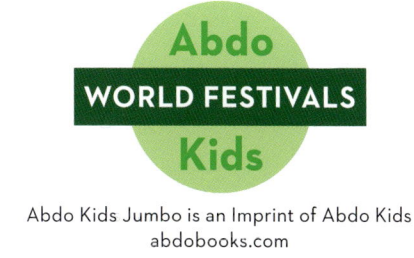

Abdo WORLD FESTIVALS Kids

Abdo Kids Jumbo is an Imprint of Abdo Kids
abdobooks.com

abdobooks.com

Published by Abdo Kids, a division of ABDO, P.O. Box 398166, Minneapolis, Minnesota 55439.
Copyright © 2023 by Abdo Consulting Group, Inc. International copyrights reserved in all countries.
No part of this book may be reproduced in any form without written permission from the publisher.
Abdo Kids Jumbo™ is a trademark and logo of Abdo Kids.

Printed in the United States of America, North Mankato, Minnesota.

102022

012023

THIS BOOK CONTAINS
RECYCLED MATERIALS

Photo Credits: Alamy, Getty Images, Granger Collection, Shutterstock

Production Contributors: Teddy Borth, Jennie Forsberg, Grace Hansen
Design Contributors: Candice Keimig, Pakou Moua

Library of Congress Control Number: 2021950559

Publisher's Cataloging-in-Publication Data

Names: Hansen, Grace, author.

Title: Harbin ice and snow festival / by Grace Hansen.

Description: Minneapolis, Minnesota : Abdo Kids, 2023 | Series: World festivals | Includes online resources
    and index.

Identifiers: ISBN 9781098261764 (lib. bdg.) | ISBN 9781098262600 (ebook) | ISBN 9781098263027
    (Read-to-Me ebook)

Subjects: LCSH: Winter festivals--Juvenile literature. | Ice sculpture--Juvenile literature. | Snow sculpture--
    Juvenile literature. | Festivals--Juvenile literature. | Harbin Shi (China)--Juvenile literature. | Manners
    and customs--Juvenile literature.

Classification: DDC 394.2683--dc23

Table of Contents

The Harbin Ice and Snow Festival

The Harbin Ice and Snow Festival is a magical occasion. It takes place in northeast China in the city of Harbin. The two-month-long event starts on January 5th each year.

Europe

Asia

China

Harbin

Africa

N
W · E
S

History

The Harbin Ice and Snow Festival's chilly origins go back to the early Qing Dynasty. Fishermen made lanterns in wintertime by placing candles inside ice blocks. The men could work longer hours along the Songhua River.

The festival was officially established in 1985. That year it merged with the Ice Lantern Show that began in 1963. In 1999, Ice and Snow World **debuted**.

Things To See and Do

The festival is known for its ice and snow **sculptures**. Beginning in December, workers cut and haul thousands of blocks of ice from the Songhua. It takes 7,000 workers two weeks to build the icy kingdom.

Many visitors flock to the remarkable site around 3:00 pm. They take in the **sculptures** in the daylight. But soon, night falls and the sculptures light up with beautiful colors.

Sun Island hosts a snow carving competition. Artists from around the world compete to create dazzling works of art.

The Harbin Show combines ice dancing, magic, and **acrobatics**. It takes place three times a day. In between, people can enjoy giant ice slides and mazes.

The Songhua River is another great site to visit. There, people like to skate and fish. The bravest ones take part in the **polar plunge**.

19

The festival is a fairy-tale wedding venue too. Brides and grooms from around the globe take part in a mass **ceremony**.

Facts and Figures

Claim to fame:
Largest ice and snow festival in the world

Opening Ceremony:
January 5

Average daily high temperature:
9 degrees F (-13 degrees C)

Ice weight hauled from river:
37 million pounds (about 17 million kg)

Number of ice-loaded truck trips:
Up to 50,000

Number of artists carving ice and snow:
10,000

Longest ice slide:
980 feet (300 meters)

Glossary

acrobatics – the art of performing gymnastic feats.

ceremony – a formal act or series of acts done in a particular way to honor a special occasion.

debuted – presented to the public for the first time.

polar plunge – an event held during the winter where participants enter a very cold body of water.

Qing Dynasty – the last imperial dynasty of China (1644-1911) founded by northeast Asian people who called themselves Manchus.

sculpture – an object made by carving, chiseling, or molding.

Index

Abdo Kids ONLINE
FREE! ONLINE MULTIMEDIA RESOURCES

Visit **abdokids.com** to access crafts, games, videos, and more!

Use Abdo Kids code **WHK1764** or scan this QR code!